Lisa D. Hoff

SAVANNAH

GEORGIA

Self-guided Tours in 88 Pictures.

SAVANNAH — Past and Present

On February 12, 1733, a small British galley with 114 settlers on board anchored at the foot of a high bluff on the Savannah River. The 40-foot-high plateau had been chosen as the site for the capital of England's 13th colonly by James Edward Oglethorpe, one of the trustees of the colony and its self-styled leader.

Oglethorpe, a member of Parliament, had conceived the idea of a new colony settled by poor people, soldiers and foreign protestants. In addition to being a haven for the poor, the new settlement was to become a defense between the prospering Carolina territories and the Spanish possessions in Florida and was to supply England with silk, flax, potash and wine. In return for free transport to the colony, 50 acres of land — including a small house lot in town — cattle and supplies, the settlers had to agree to stay in Georgia for at least three years, to plant 500 white mulberry trees and to contribute to the defense of the colony.

Confronted with problems they were ill-equipped to cope with and a wilderness rather than a promised land, disillusioned settlers soon began to leave Georgia for the Carolinas where they were not prohibited from owning slaves and land, and from drinking and selling rum. In 1743, Oglethorpe, returning to England for good, left behind a dispirited and much reduced colony. The final blow came when, in 1751, Parliament cut off all funds for the 13th colony. One year later the Trustees surrendered their charter to the crown.

Savannah's first boom was based on the cultivation of rice, a labor-intensive business which required slaves, since the watery swamps were not considered "fit for a white man to work." Within 15 years after the trustees' antislavery law was overturned, in 1750, the total slave population of the colony rose to 16,000. A new class of rice planters and shipping merchants built huge estates and elegant town homes. Warehouses and wharves along the Bay held rice, indigo, timber, pelts and the first bales of a new crop, cotton, destined for Bristol or Liverpool.

During the last years of the British venture in the New World, Savannah was a divided city. While the old colonists staunchly defended the royal governor and British laws, their sons met in Tondee's Tavern to discuss sedition, self-determination, boycott and liberty. On August 10, 1776, the Liberty Boys and excited Savannahians celebrated the Declaration of Independence with a mock funeral cortege for King George.

Two years later, the British recaptured Savannah in one day and Georgia became again a British royal province, although some parts of the interior and lower coast remained in the hands of the rebels. In October 1779, a French fleet under Charles Comte d'Estaing disembarked over four thousand troops. They were soon joined by American forces from Charleston and Georgia militia from Augusta. Their failed attempt to recapture Savannah remains one of the bloodiest battles of the Revolution. Savannah's liberation finally came in 1782.

The invention of the cotton gin by a young schoolteacher from New Haven, Eli Whitney, transformed Savannah into a world port. In 1790, cotton exports were 1,000 bales; thirty years later they were 90,000 bales, and in 1840, they had soared to 408,000 bales a year.

On the eve of the Civil War, the city had a population of 14,000. Majestic mansions and graceful row houses gave the new streets near Forsyth Park an air of prosperity and elegance. Three railroad lines transported cotton and timber from the Georgia midlands to the wharves on the Savannah River.

On January 19, 1861, Georgia became the fifth state to secede from the United States. Savannah felt invincible, since two weeks earlier a small band of volunteers had captured Fort Pulaski on the mouth of the Savannah River. A year later when the Union recaptured the fort, Savannahians began to realize that the Union blockade of their port was the end of commerce and business, and that the English and French did not miss cotton enough to come to their aid. Stores closed, wharves remained empty and only rare blockade runners docked on River Street. Except for the troops stationed in Savannah, the city would have become a ghost town. After the Battle of Atlanta, 9,000 graycoats waited in Savannah for the Union army of 70,000. When it became apparent that all supply routes to Savannah were in the hands of the enemy, they abandoned the defense of the city, and Savannah surrendered.

The Civil War left Savannah a defeated city. The beautiful squares and mansions looked shabby, the harbor was blocked by scuttled Confederate ships, the railroads were destroyed, there were no jobs, no food, no money.

By 1883, Savannah was sufficiently recovered to celebrate the sesquicentennial with electric lights, streetcars, some indoor plumbing, and best of all, a newly opened Cotton Exchange which soon was dubbed the "Wall Street of the South." The city expanded south of Gaston Street, adding the Victorian District with its "gingerbread" architecture to Savannah's many styles. On weekends, Savannahians either took the new railroad to Tybee Beach, or went to band concerts in Forsyth Park, or to yacht and horse races. The newly dredged river channel made Savannah a major port on the Atlantic coast.

World War I dramatically changed the tranquil city, as Savannah's port became a major port of embarkation. This was continued in World War II, when from Hunter Army Airfield, just outside the city, the huge bombers of the famed Eighth Air Force took off to crush Hitler's forces.

After the war, Savannah became again a decaying city, and many of the stately homes were turned into shabby slum tenements. However in the 1950's, something happened that shocked Savannah into action. The old City Market was demolished to make room for a parking garage. Outraged citizens got together to save the historic district before it was lost to the wrecking ball. In 1966, the National Park Service designated a two and one half mile area as a Registered National Landmark.

During the Centennial Olympic Games in 1996, Savannah will draw world-wide attention. The Olympic yachting events will be staged in the Atlantic Ocean, and beach volleyball, a first-time Olympic sport, will attract some 8,000 spectators to nearby Tybee Island.

Acknowledgements:

My thanks are due to:

Mrs. Anna Decristoforo
Mrs. Robert L. Heriot,
    St. John's Church Parish House
Mr. J. Edward Jackson,
    Coastal Heritage Society
Ms. Minnie Matilde Miles,
    King-Tisdell Cottage Foundation, Inc.
Ms. Jenny Stacy,
    Savannah Area Convention & Visitor's Bureau
Mrs. Elisabeth Torggler Schäfer

Print and photographs courtesy of:

Georgia Historical Society, print, page 2
Juliette Gordon Low Girl Scout National Center, page 13, photo by Tim Rhoad
Robert L. Heriot, page 19
Savannah Area Convention & Visitor's Bureau, pages 20 and 30
The Andrew Low House, page 29
Telfair Academy of Arts and Sciences, Inc., page 37, photo by Daniel L. Grantham, Jr.
Coastal Heritage Society, pages 42 and 43, photos by John Carter
Ships of the Sea Maritime Museum, page 53, photo by Craig Stevens
King-Tisdell Cottage Foundation, Inc., page 54
Coastal Heritage Society, page 57, photo by Steve Roberson
Golden Isles Visitor's Bureau, pages 63 and 64

SAVANNAH - HIER ET AUJOURD'HUI

Le 12 février 1733, un petit navire britannique avec à son bord 114 colons vint jeter l'ancre au pied d'une haute falaise de la rivière Savannah. Ce plateau de quelque 12 mètres d'altitude avait été choisi comme site de la capitale de la 13e colonie de l'Angleterre par James Edward Oglethorpe, l'un des administrateurs de la colonie et son dirigeant de fait.

Oglethorpe, qui était membre du Parlement, avait conçu cette idée d'une colonie composée de pauvres, de soldats et de protestants étrangers. Cette terre d'accueil des plus démunis devait aussi servir de défense entre les territoires prospères des Carolines et les possessions espagnoles de la Floride, et approvisionner l'Angleterre en soie, lin, potasse et vin. Et en échange pour leur transport gratuit jusqu'au site de la colonie, plus 20 hectares de terres -y compris une petite parcelle à bâtir en ville-, du bétail et des provisions, les colons devaient s'engager à rester en Géorgie pendant au moins trois ans, pendant lesquels ils devaient planter 500 mûriers blancs et assurer la défense de leur colonie.

Mais, confrontés à des difficultés qu'ils ne savaient comment résoudre et à une nature sauvage plutôt qu'à un paradis, les colons commencèrent bientôt à quitter la Géorgie pour les Carolines, où nul ne leur interdisait d'avoir des esclaves, d'être propriétaires de leurs terres et de boire et vendre du rhum. En 1743, Oglethorpe s'embarqua une dernière fois pour l'Angleterre, laissant derrière lui une colonie bien réduite et déçue. Le coup de grâce survint lorsqu'en 1751 Le Parlement cessa entièrement de financer la 13e colonie. Un an plus tard, ses administrateurs en abandonnèrent la charte au royaume.

La première explosion de Savannah fut basée sur la culture du riz, une entreprise à forte intensité de main d'oeuvre exigeant l'utilisation d'esclaves, car les marécages n'étaient pas considérés comme „terrains où l'homme blanc pouvait s'abaisser à travailler". En 1750, quinze ans après l'abrogation de la loi antiesclavagiste adoptée par les

administrateurs de la colonie, la population totale d'esclaves de la colonie atteignit les 16.000 âmes. Une nouvelle classe sociale de planteurs de riz et d'armateurs et expéditeurs vint construire d'élégantes résidences urbaines et d'immenses domaines. Entrepôts et dépôts maritimes le long de la baie stockaient le riz, l'indigo, le bois de construction, les fourrures et les premières balles d'une récolte toute nouvelle, le coton, marchandises destinées à Bristol et Liverpool.

Au cours des dernières années de la colonisation britannique du nouveau monde, Savannah devint une ville divisée. Alors que les anciens colons défendaient corps et âme le gouverneur du roi et les lois britanniques, leurs fils se retrouvaient dans la Taverne de Tondee pour parler sédition, auto-détermination, boycott et liberté. Le 10 août 1776, les Fils de la Liberté et des citoyens enflammés célébrèrent la Déclaration d'Indépendance avec un simulacre de cortège funéraire pour le roi George.

Deux ans plus tard, les Britannique reprirent Savannah en un jour et la Géorgie redevint une province du Royaume britannique, bien que certaines des régions intérieures et des basses terres demeurent entre les mains des rebelles. En octobre 1779, une flottille française sous les ordres de Charles, Comte d'Estaing, débarqua 4.000 soldats, auxquels se joignirent rapidement des troupes américaines de Charleston et de la milice géorgienne d'Augusta. Leur tentative de reconquête de Savannah se solda par un échec après l'un des épisodes les plus sanglants de la Révolution. Savannah fut enfin libérée en 1782.

L'invention de l'égreneuse de coton par un jeune professeur de New Haven, Eli Whitney, transforma Savannah en un centre portuaire mondial. En 1790, les exportations de coton se chiffraient à 1.000 balles ; trente ans plus tard, elles étaient de 90.000 balles et en 1840 elles atteignirent le chiffre record de 408.000 balles par an.

A l'aube de la guerre de Sécession, la ville avait une

population de 14.000 personnes. Des manoirs majestueux et de gracieuses résidences donnaient aux nouvelles rues de Forsyth Park un air de prospérité et d'élégance. Trois voies ferrées assuraient le transport du coton et du bois de construction entre le coeur de la Géorgie et les ports sur la rivière Savannah.

Le 19 janvier 1861, la Géorgie devint le cinquième état à faire sécession. Savannah se sentait invincible, car deux semaines plus tôt, une petite bande de volontaires avait réussi à recapturer Fort Pulaski, à l'embouchure de la rivière Savannah. Un an plus tard, lorsque les troupes du Nord reprirent le fort, les habitants de la ville commencèrent à comprendre que le blocus de leur port mettait un terme aux affaires et au commerce, et que pour les Anglais et les Français, le coton n'était pas une denrée assez précieuse pour qu'ils viennent à leur secours. Les magasins fermèrent, les docks restèrent vides et seuls de rares navires ayant percé le blocus venaient s'amarrer le long de River Street. A l'exception des troupes postées à Savannah, la ville devenait une ville fantôme. Après la bataille d'Atlanta, 9.000 tuniques grises attendirent à Savannah l'arrivée des 70.000 hommes des armées nordistes. Lorsqu'il devint évident que toutes les routes d'approvisionnement de la ville étaient tombées aux mains de l'ennemi, les soldats abandonnèrent Savannah et la ville se rendit.

La guerre de Sécession laissa Savannah en pleine détresse, ses beaux quartiers et ses manoirs majestueux avaient perdu toute leur superbe, le port restait bloqué par les navires sabordés, le chemin de fer avait été détruit, il n'y avait plus ni argent, ni travail, ni nourriture.

Quand arriva 1883, Savannah avait suffisamment recouvré de la guerre pour célébrer son cent cinquantième anniversaire avec des lampes électriques, des tramways, quelques installations de plomberie intérieure et, surtout, une nouvelle Bourse du Coton qui devint rapidement la „Wall Street du Sud". La ville s'étendit au sud de Gaston Street, avec l'adjonction du quartier victorien et de son architecture de style „maisons de pain d'épice" aux nombreux styles y existant déjà. En fin de semaine, les habitants de la ville empruntaient le nouveau chemin de fer pour se rendre à Tybee Beach, venaient entendre divers orchestres jouant dans Forsyth Park ou se rendaient aux courses de voile ou de chevaux. Le canal récemment creusé fit de Savannah l'une des principales installations portuaires sur l'océan Atlantique.

La première Guerre mondiale affecta profondément cette cité tranquille, car le port de Savannah devint l'un des principaux points d'embarquement. Cela continua lors de la deuxième Guerre mondiale, lorsque les énormes bombardiers de la célèbre huitième escadrille de l'aviation américaine s'envolèrent de l'aéroport militaire de Hunter, situé aux abords de la ville, pour aller écraser les armées hitlériennes.

Après la guerre, Savannah redevint une ville en plein marasme, et nombre de ses résidences majestueuses furent transformées en taudis sordides. Mais les années cinquante produisirent un sursaut de la ville. Les anciennes Halles de la ville furent démolies en vue de construire à leur place un parking. Outrés, les citoyens se rassemblèrent pour sauver le quartier historique avant qu'il ne devienne la proie des démolisseurs. En 1966, le National Park Service désigna monument historique un quartier de près de 6,5 kilomètres carrés.

Lors des Jeux Olympiques du Centenaire, en 1996, Savannah sera à nouveau le centre de l'attention mondiale. En effet, les épreuves olympiques de voile seront disputées sur l'océan Atlantique, et les compétitions de volley-ball de plage, discipline olympique pour la première fois de son histoire, attireront plus de 8.000 spectateurs sur l'île voisine de Tybee.

DIE GESCHICHTE DER STADT SAVANNAH.

Am 12. Februar 1733 ankerte ein kleines Schiff mit 114 Siedlern am Fuße eines steilen Ufers im Fluß "Savannah". James Edward Oglethorpe, einer der Treuhänder der Kolonie und ihr selbsternannter Leiter, hatte dieses erhöhte Plateau als Sitz der Hauptstadt der 13. Kolonie Englands gewählt.

Oglethorpe, ein englisches Parlamentsmitglied, hatte die Absicht, diese Kolonie mit den Ärmsten Englands, mit Soldaten und mit ausländischen Protestanten zu besiedeln. Dadurch wollte er zwei Ziele erreichen, ein Paradies für die Armen und Verfolgten, gleichzeitig aber auch einen Pufferstaat zwischen den wohlhabenden, englischen Kolonien im Norden und den spanischen Besitzungen in Florida zu schaffen. Außerdem sollte die neue Kolonie England mit Seide, Flachs, Potasche und Wein versorgen. Als Gegenleistung für die Überfahrt, für 20 Hektar Land, Vieh und Werkzeuge mußte sich jeder Kolonist verpflichten, mindestens drei Jahre in Georgia zu bleiben, 500 Maulbeerbäume zu pflanzen und die Kolonie gegen die Spanier zu verteidigen.

Die Stadt, die Oglethorpe auf der Ebene oberhalb des Flusses anlegte, teilte er in gleiche Bezirke ein, die jeweils einen großen Platz umgaben. Ein Jahr nach seiner Ankunft berichtete Oglethorpe, daß bereits 467 Leute die Unterstützung der Treuhänder genossen.

Enttäuschte Siedler, die mit den unerwarteten Schwierigkeiten in Georgia nicht fertig wurden, begannen jedoch schon bald die Kolonie zu verlassen. Sie fanden Südkarolina, wo die Einfuhr von Sklaven, der Verkauf von Alkohol und Privateigentum an Grund und Boden erlaubt waren, vielversprechender. Als Oglethorpe 1743 nach England zurückkehrte, ließ er eine mutlose und sehr verkleinerte Gruppe zurück. Die größte Enttäuschung kam mit der Weigerung des Parlaments, Georgia weiterhin finanziell zu unterstützen. 1752 wurde Georgia eine königliche Kolonie.

Savannahs erster Aufschwung wurde durch den Anbau von Reis hervorgerufen. Da Reis ein sehr arbeitsintensives Produkt ist, und man glaubte, daß die Sümpfe für Weiße ungesund seien, erlaubte das englische Parlament die Einfuhr von Sklaven. Innerhalb von 15 Jahren nach Abschaffung des Antisklavengesetzes stieg die Anzahl der Sklaven auf 16.000. Eine neue Bevölkerungsschichte von reichen Plantagen- und Reedereibesitzern errichtete großartige Ansitze und elegante Stadthäuser. Die Kais, Piers und Lager waren vollgestopft mit Reis, Indigo, Holz und einem neuen Produkt, Baumwolle.

In den letzten Jahren der englischen Kolonialzeit war Savannah eine geteilte Stadt. Während die alten Kolonisten hartnäckig die englischen Gouverneure und die englischen Gesetze verteidigten, redeten ihre Söhne in Tondees Taverne von Meuterei, Selbstbestimmung, Boykott und Freiheit. Am 10. August 1776 feierten die "Freiheitsburschen" und die Bevölkerung von Savannah die Unabhängigkeitserklärung der Vereinigten Staaten mit einem Scheinleichenzug für den englischen König.

Zwei Jahre später wurde Georgia wieder eine königliche Provinz. Im Oktober 1779 landete Graf d'Estaing mit einer französischen Flotte von 4.000 Soldaten. Verstärkt durch amerikanische Truppen und Georgia Miliz griffen sie Savannah an. Dieser Versuch, die Stadt zurückzuerobern, ist eine der blutigsten Schlachten der Amerikanischen Revolution. 1782 wurde Savannah dann endlich frei.

Die Erfindung der Baumwollegreniermaschine durch einen jungen Lehrer aus New Haven namens Eli Whitney verwandelt Savannah in eine Welthafenstadt. 1790 wurden 1.000 Ballen Baumwolle exportiert, 30 Jahre später waren es

90.000, und 1840 wurden 408.000 Ballen in alle Welt verschickt. Das Jahr 1819 war Savannahs Höhepunkt: Präsident Monroe kam zu einem offiziellen Besuch, die amerikanische Bank eröffnete eine ihrer ersten Branchen, ein junger Engländer, William Jay, begann architektonische Meisterwerke für Savannahs Elite zu bauen, und das Dampfschiff "Savannah" überquerte den Atlantik in einer Rekordzeit von 29 Tagen und 11 Stunden. Das darauffolgende Jahr war katastrophal, zwei Drittel der Häuser brannten ab, und Gelbfieber reduzierte die Einwohnerzahl um ein Zehntel.

Zu Beginn des Bürgerkrieges zählte Savannah 14.000 Einwohner. Die neuen Straßen um den Forsyth Park mit ihren großartigen Villen und anmutigen Häuserreihen erweckten den Eindruck von Eleganz und Wohlstand. Drei Eisenbahnlinien transportierten Baumwolle und Holzprodukte von Mittelgeorgia zu den Werften Savannahs.

Am 19. Jänner 1861 wurde Georgia der fünfte Staat, der aus der Union austrat. Savannah glaubte sich unbesiegbar nach der Eroberung des Forts Pulaski an der Mündung des Savannahflusses durch Freiwillige zwei Wochen zuvor. Nach der Wiedereroberung der Festung durch die Unionssoldaten wurde bereits ein Jahr später klar, daß mit der Blockade Savannahs der Exporthandel zu Ende war und daß weder England noch Frankreich dem Süden zu Hilfe kommen würden. Geschäfte mußten zusperren, Werften und Lager standen leer und mit Ausnahme der seltenen Blockadebrecher dockten keine Schiffe an River Street. Ohne das Militär wäre Savannah eine Geisterstadt geworden. 9.000 Soldaten in grauen Uniformen warteten nach der Schlacht von Atlanta auf die 70.000 Mann starke Armee der Union. Doch als alle Nachschubrouten abgeschnitten waren, gaben die Südstaatler die Verteidigung der Stadt auf, und Savannah kapitulierte.

Nach dem Bürgerkrieg lag Savannah am Boden, der Hafen war durch gesunkene Kriegsschiffe unbrauchbar, die Eisenbahn war zerstört, die eleganten Häuser waren halb verfallen, und es gab weder Arbeit, Nahrungsmittel, noch Geld.

1883 hatte sich Savannah von der Verwüstung bereits soweit erholt, daß die Stadt die 150-Jahrfeier ihrer Gründung mit elektrischen Straßenlampen und einer neuen Straßenbahn feiern konnte. Eine Börse für Baumwolle verwandelte Bay Street in die Wallstreet des Südens. Die Stadt wuchs, und die neuen Häuser im viktorianischen Zuckerbäckerstil brachten Abwechslung in Savannahs Baukultur. Am Wochenende fuhren die Einwohner mit der neuen Eisenbahn nach Tybee Island, oder sie besuchten Konzerte im Park, Segelwettbewerbe oder Pferderennen.

Im ersten Weltkrieg wurde der ruhige Hafen Savannahs einer der bedeutendsten Kriegshäfen der USA. Diese Tradition wurde im zweiten Weltkrieg fortgesetzt, nun waren es jedoch die Bomber der Achten Luftwaffe, die Savannah bekannt machten.

Nach dem Krieg verwandelten sich viele der einst schönen Wohnviertel in schmutzige Elendsviertel. In den fünfziger Jahren wurden die Bewohner Savannahs allerdings plötzlich aus ihrer Lethargie aufgeschreckt. Der Abbruch des alten städtischen Marktes, der einer Hochgarage Platz machte, veranlaßte die Bürger, sich zusammenzutun, um ihre historischen Gebäude zu retten. 1966 wurde das innere Stadtgebiet unter Denkmalschutz gestellt.

Savannah wird 1996 die Aufmerksamkeit der ganzen Welt auf sich ziehen. Bei den Olympischen Sommerspielen werden die Segelwettbewerbe im Atlantik vor Savannah abgehalten, und Strandvolleyball, das zum ersten Mal ein olympischer Sport wird, wird 8.000 Zuschauer nach Tybee Island locken.

サバンナ － 過去と現在

1733年2月12日、入植者114名を乗せた英国の小型帆船が、サバンナ川に面した崖のふもとに錨を下ろした。高さ12メートルの崖の上に広がる台地が、英国の13番目の植民地となることに決まっていた。この植民地の自治体の一員、ジェームズ・エドワード・オグルソープが、自ら植民地の指導者となった。

英議会員だったオグルソープは、貧民、兵士、そして外国人新教徒による新しい植民地の構想を抱いていた。このジョージア植民地は、貧しい者の新天地となるとともに、すでに栄えていたカロライナ植民地と、フロリダのスペイン属領地との間で防御地帯の役割を果たし、さらに英国向けの絹、亜麻、ワインなどを産出することが期待されていた。

サバンナ川を見下ろす崖の上にオグルソープが築いた町は、いくつかの区に分けられ、各区の中央には広場があった。どの広場にも、公共の建物や教会の敷地となる信託地が用意された。

しかし、入植者たちを待っていたのは、希望の地ではなく、厳しい荒野だった。手に負えないような問題が次々と発生した。失望した入植者たちは、まもなくジョージアを去り始め、土地と奴隷の所有やラム酒の飲用・販売が許されているカロライナへ移っていった。1743年、オグルソープが本国へ帰る頃には、残された植民地は当初の活気が失われ、規模もかなり縮小されていた。1751年には、英議会がジョージア植民地への資金援助をすべて打ち切り、1年後、植民地自治体は国王に自治権を返還した。

サバンナに初めて発展の機会をもたらしたのは、米の栽培だった。米作は労働集約型の農業であり、しかも米が栽培される湿地は「白人が働くにはふさわしくない土地」とされていたため、黒人奴隷の使用が不可欠だった。自治体が定めた奴隷禁止法は1750年に廃止され、その後15年間で植民地内の奴隷人口は16,000人に達した。農園主や海運業者が新たな富裕階級を形成し、巨大な農園や優雅な邸宅を建設した。湾沿いに立ち並んだ倉庫や埠頭には、ブリストルやリバプールへ向けて出荷される米、藍、材木、毛皮、綿花などが山積みにされていた。

英国による新世界進出時代の末期、サバンナの町は二派に分かれた。古い入植者たちが、英国王遣の総督と英国の法律を断固支持したのに対し、その息子の世代は、反乱、植民地の自決、ボイコット、自由といったことを話し合っていた。1776年8月10日、独立派の「リバティ・ボーイズ」を先頭に、サバンナの住民は、国王ジョージ三世の「葬送行列」の真似をして、独立宣言採択を祝った。

しかし、その2年後、英国はわずか1日でサバンナを再び占領し、ジョージアは英国の植民地に戻った。1779年10月、フランス艦隊が4,000を超える軍勢をサバンナに上陸させた。これにチャールストンのアメリカ軍とジョージアのオーガスタから派遣された市民軍が参加して、サバ

ンナ奪還を図り、独立戦争でも屈指の激戦を繰り広げたが、奪還は成らなかった。サバンナがようやく解放されるのは、1782年のことである。

南北戦争直前のサバンナの人口は14,000人だった。フォーサイス公園周辺の新しい通りには、豪華な邸宅や優美な続き住宅が建てられ、栄華の空気を漂わせていた。ジョージア内陸部とサバンナを結ぶ3本の鉄道が、綿花や材木をサバンナ川沿いの埠頭へ運んできた。

1861年1月19日、ジョージア州は、米国連邦から脱退する5番目の州となった。その2週間前、サバンナでは、少数の義勇兵がサバンナ川河口のプラスキ砦を占領し、士気を昂揚させていた。しかし、1年後に北軍が同砦を再び攻略し、港湾を封鎖すると、サバンナ市民は通商の道を断たれた。そして英国もフランスも援軍を送るほど綿花輸入を重視していないことを思い知らされた。サバンナ市内の商店は閉ざされ、埠頭は空になり、まれに封鎖を破って入港してきた船が見られるのみとなった。市内に駐屯する兵士たちがいなければ、サバンナはゴーストタウンと言ってもよかった。アトランタの戦いで勝利を収めた北軍は、7万人の大軍で海へ向かって進軍してきた。これを迎え撃つべくサバンナで待機していた南軍兵は、わずか9,000人だった。補給路をすべて北軍に押さえられたことを知った南軍は、サバンナ防衛をあきらめ、降伏した。

南北戦争で敗戦都市となったサバンナでは、美しかった広場や大邸宅は荒れ果て、港には沈没した南軍の船が放置され、鉄道は破壊され、仕事も財産も失った住民は、食べ物にも困る状態だった。

しかし、1883年、入植150周年を迎える頃には、サバンナの復興も進み、電気、市電、下水設備なども登場していた。中でも、新設の綿花取引所は、「南部のウォール・ストリート」と呼ばれるほどの活況を呈した。また、河川水路の浚渫が新たに行われ、サバンナ港は米国大西洋岸有数の港湾となった。

第一次世界大戦中は、サバンナ港が主要乗船港となったため、静かな町が一変した。続いて第二次世界大戦でも、サバンナ郊外のハンター陸軍飛行場から、有名な第8航空軍の大爆撃機が欧州戦線へ飛び立って行った。

戦後、サバンナの町は再び衰退し、壮麗な邸宅の多くは、荒れ果てたスラムと化した。しかし、1950年代に、市民が立ち上がって歴史地区保存運動を始め、全長4キロメートルにわたる歴史地区が、国定保存建造物の指定を受けた。

1996年、アトランタで開催されるオリンピック100周年記念大会では、サバンナも世界の注目を集める。同大会のヨット競技が、大西洋沿岸のスキダウェイ島で開催されるほか、タイビー島ではオリンピック競技として初めて取り入れられるビーチ・バレーボールの試合が行われ、約8,000人の観客を集める予定である。

Savannah seen from Hutchinson Island. In February, 1733, the ship *Anne* with 114 settlers on board anchored at the foot of Yamacraw Bluff. James Oglethorpe, representing the Trustees of the new colony, had selected the forty-foot high plateau which looked out over the Savannah River and the surrounding marshes as the site of their settlement. Oglethorpe had conceived the town as a series of squares which were each surrounded by trust lots for public buildings and tithing lots for settlers' cottages. The town was to be named after the river Savannah.

By the time Fermin Cerveau painted this panorama, in 1837, Whitney's invention of the cotton gin had revitalized the languishing cultivation of cotton and turned Savannah into a flourishing trading center. In the 1830's, 18 of the 24 squares had been built, and the city extended almost to the present boundaries of Historic Savannah.

River Street became the bustling center of commerce. Warehouses and naval stores were built at the foot of the bluff, tall enough to rise several levels above Bay Street. The upper levels, which were used as offices for the brokers, were connected to Bay Street by wooden bridges and cast iron arches. The ramps leading from Bay Street level down the bluff to River Street were paved with stones brought as ballast in early sailing ships.

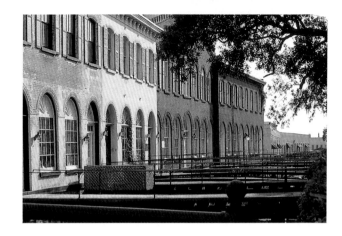

Factors Walk. During the eighteenth century, factors and traders had conducted their business from the decks of ships and the wharfs along the river. The first offices/warehouses, Commerce Row, were built on the west side of Bay Street, followed by Factors Row which was named for the cotton factors, or brokers, who brought fame and prosperity to nineteenth century Savannah with their flair for cotton commerce and for lavish lifestyles.

When the Cotton Exchange was built cotton exports produced revenues of $40 million and the area was known as the "Wall Street of the South." The Exchange's Board of Trade did not only fix the price of cotton but also of the newly developed money crops, turpentine and resin.

The U.S. Custom House, completed in 1852, stands on the site of the house Oglethorpe rented. He never built a house for himself in the new colony although he stayed until 1743. Architect John S. Norris, who had come to Savannah to design the Custom House, had the 15-ton columns shipped to Savannah from Quincey, Massachusetts.

City Hall (1906) stands on the site of the former City Exchange. The City Exchange was Savannah's first major building and served as the headquarters for government, business, state affairs and entertainment throughout the entire nineteenth century.

Johnson Square was the first square to be laid out and named by Oglethorpe. Today it represents the financial center of Savannah. In Oglethorpe's design it was to be the economic center with its Trustees' Store where all supplies were issued to the settlers, the Publick Oven and Mill and a House for Strangers. Oglethorpe named the square after Governor Robert Johnson of South Carolina whose protection and help was constantly needed. The marble obelisk pays tribute to and marks the grave of General Nathanael Greene, Revolutionary War hero.

Christ Episcopal Church on Johnson Square is the only church in Savannah which was specified in Oglethorpe's plan. Before the Revolution, Christ Church parish served as the center for the twelve parishes into which the colony was divided. Both John Wesley and George Whitefield were ministers of Christ Church. The present church was rebuilt within the original walls after the fire of 1898.

Wright Square was named after the third and last royal governor in Georgia (1760-1782). Under James Wright's governorship Georgia prospered and Wright was soon named "His Majesty's most able Administrator in the Americas." He was also an able business man for he soon became one of the wealthiest planters in Georgia. In 1776, Wright was put under house arrest but managed to escape to England. The Gordon Monument was erected to honor Savannah's railroad pioneer, for the Central of Georgia Railroad, built 1833-43, brought not only cotton to Savannah but also huge profits.

This stone was dedicated to the memory of Tomochichi, chief of the Yamacraw Indians, who was Oglethorpe's and the colonists' friend, benefactor and ally. An intelligent, kind, dignified and perceptive man, Tomochichi realised that his people and the white colonists could build a better future for both through friendship and peace. At his instigation the Creek tribes and Oglethorpe signed a treaty in which land was granted to the colony and boundaries were set in return for special trade provisions. Tomochichi was buried in Wright Square, then the center of town, with military honors.

Juliette Gordon Low Birthplace. Juliette "Daisy" Gordon Low, the founder of the Girl Scouts of the U.S.A., was born in this William Jay designed house in 1860. At the age of 26, the headstrong and eccentric Savannah belle married the only son of a wealthy British cotton factor, William Low. Daisy Low plunged into the British social scene with the same verve and savoir faire which characterized her earlier life and soon she introduced London society to Southern food such as grits, ham and sweet potatoes and set new fashion trends with her elegant Paris originals.

At age 52, Daisy returned to Savannah to found the first Girl Guide troop which was patterned after the British Guides and consisted of eighteen girls. In 1913, they became the Girl Scouts. As the Girl Scout movement became established, Juliette Low began to devote herself to the international aspects of Girl Scouts. By the time of her death in 1927, Girl Scouts of the U.S.A. had grown to 167,925 members. The Juliette Gordon Low House became Savannah's first National Historic Landmark and it serves as the Girl Scouts National Center.

The Independent Presbyterian Church, dedicated in 1819, replaced the first Independent Presbyterian Church on Bryan Street which had exerted influence on the history of Savannah during the Revolution. The Reverend John Joachim Zubly, one of the most persuasive preachers in the province, spoke so powerfully about freedom from oppression that all of Savannah came to hear his sermons. The Independent Presbyterian Church burned in 1889 but was immediately rebuilt by William Holden Green of Rhode Island who reportedly had been inspired by St. Martin-in-the-Fields in London.

Chippewa Square (1815) commemorates the Canadian Battle of Chippewa in the War of 1812. It was the center of Savannah's glittering nightlife. William Jay's Savannah Theatre, which became the symbol of the city's new prosperity and elegance, stood on the northeast corner of the square until it burned in 1948. The First Baptist Church, built in 1833, still stands as Savannah's oldest church.

The statue of General James Edward Oglethorpe, founder of the colony of Georgia and Savannah, its capital, is facing south "ever on guard against the Spaniards." King George II had given his approval to the new colony only after the Trustees had convinced him that Georgia would act as the southern buffer between thriving South Carolina and Spain which claimed most of the unsettled wilderness between St. Augustine and the Altamaha River.

Madison Square. After the two "War of 1812" squares, Orleans and Chippewa, the prosperity of Savannah was interrupted by a devastating fire, a yellow fever epidemic and a national depression which delayed development until 1837, when Madison (named for President James Madison), Lafayette and Pulaski Squares were created. The monument in the middle of the square is for Sergeant William Jasper, hero of the siege of Savannah in 1779, who died while attempting to save his unit flag. St. John's Church was built in 1852 and is treasured for its beautiful chimes and stained glass windows.

The Green-Meldrim House (1853) was designed by John S. Norris for Charles Green, a prosperous Englishman and cotton broker. The house, considered to be the "Finest Gothic Revival house south of Virginia," cost $93,000 to construct and was possibly the most expensive house built in antebellum Savannah. It was the first home with indoor plumbing and a domed stair with a removable skylight. Edward Green sold the house in 1892 to Judge Peter Meldrim. It remained in the Meldrim family until 1943 when the adjacent St. John Episcopal Church acquired it for its parish house.

When General Sherman reached Savannah, Green offered him his spacious home as his headquarters. Sherman and his army entered Savannah on December 22, 1864, after the Confederate army, cut off from reinforcements, retreated into South Carolina. The city surrendered and Sherman sent his famous telegram to President Lincoln: "I beg to present you as a Christmas Gift, the City of Savannah. . ." From the Green-Meldrim house Sherman issued his Field Order 16, granting "40 acres and a mule" to newly freed black citizens. While in Savannah, Sherman slept in this bedroom.

Mercer-Wilder House on Monterey Square. Monterey Square (1847) was named to memorialize the capture of Monterey, Mexico, in 1846 by General Zachary Taylor. The Mercer-Wilder house was designed by John S. Norris in 1860. It was the ancestral home of songwriter, Johnny Mercer, a winner of four Grammy popular song awards and one Oscar. The Pulaski Monument honors the memory of Count Casimir Pulaski, the gallant Polish adventurer who was Washington's first cavalry commander and financier. He was mortally wounded in a cavalry charge in the Battle of Savannah in 1779.

The Temple Mickve Israel, the only Gothic synagogue in America, was built in 1776-78. America's third oldest Jewish congregation was founded five months after the colonization of Georgia when a ship with 42 Jews arrived in Savannah's port. Oglethorpe welcomed the newcomers in spite of the trustees' opposition to Jewish settlers. Among the new arrivals was a renowned Portuguese physician, Dr. Samuel Nunez, whom Oglethorpe credited with saving the colony from a fever epidemic. The museum adjoining the temple houses priceless books, letters and artifacts.

Forsyth Park was laid out in 1851 and named for John Forsyth, minister to Spain, governor of Georgia and secretary of state under Presidents Andrew Jackson and Martin Van Buren. Public parks were the vogue then, and Savannah hired William Bischoff of Bavaria to landscape the park. The 1875 Confederate Monument in Forsyth Park Extension, which was originally the military parade ground, is surrounded by the busts of Brigadier General Francis S. Bartow and General Lafayette MacLaws, both Confederate heroes. To the south is the Spanish-American War Memorial.

The Fountain in Forsyth Park was believed to be the largest in the nation when it was unveiled in 1858. The design of the fountain was taken from one exhibited at the Crystal Palace in 1851. An identical fountain with an Indian maiden on top stands in Cuzco, Peru. To the right of the fountain is the Fragrant Garden for the Blind which was planted by Savannah garden clubs.

Entrances to typical Savannah row houses.

Calhoun Square (1851) was named after John C. Calhoun from South Carolina who, as Secretary of War, accompanied President Monroe to Savannah on the occasion of the launching of the *S.S. Savannah*, the first steamship to cross the Atlantic in 1819. In 1856, Massie Common School, Savannah's first city-operated elementary school, was built as a legacy by a Scottish immigrant, Peter Massie of Brunswick. Today it houses the Massie Heritage Interpretation Center of the Savannah-Chatham Public Schools.

Wesley Monumental Methodist Church. John and Charles Wesley, the later founders of Methodism, arrived in Savannah in 1736. Charles stayed in Georgia for only one year. He spent most of that time as Oglethorpe's secretary in Frederica on St. Simon's Island. John Wesley was a zealous young man intent to convert the Indians and to minister the gospel to the colonists. Two years after his landing at Cockspur Island, he returned to England a changed and chastened man. The Wesley Monumental Methodist Church was built in their honor and features the famous Wesley Window.

The Andrew Low House (1849) was built by distinguished architect John Norris for the English cotton merchant Andrew Low who was one of the wealthiest men in the British Empire. Andrew Low had come to Savannah in the 1830's as a young man to join his uncle in his export/brokerage firm. While staying with the Lows during a lecture tour, the English novelist, William M. Thackeray, described the lifestyle of the Savannah cotton brokers, "They are tremendous men, these cotton merchants."

Juliette Gordon Low who had married William Low, Andrew's son, lived in the house after her return to the United States until her death in 1927. She willed the carriage house to the Savannah chapter of the Girl Scouts. The mansion is now owned and preserved by the National Society of the Colonial Dames in Georgia and is open as a museum.

The Hamilton-Turner House was built in 1873 for Samuel Pugh Hamilton, jeweler and prominent citizen. This Savannah townhouse is a good example of the Second Empire style which was popular from 1855 to 1885. Lafayette Square (1837) was named for Marquis de Lafayette who visitied Savannah in 1825 to dedicate the monument in Johnson Square to his revolutionary friend, Nathanael Greene. The writer, Flannery O'Connor (her house is open to the public), grew up on Lafayette Square during the Depression. She attended the nearby Catholic School.

The cathedral St. John the Baptist is the oldest Roman Catholic church in Georgia and the seat of the Diocese of Savannah. The charter for the new colony excluded Catholics from among God's oppressed who were invited to come to "the most delightful country of the universe." The first Catholic immigrants were 200 Scottish Highlanders who arrived as early as 1735 and who founded the town of Darien.

The original French Gothic cathedral was dedicated in 1876, destroyed by fire 22 years later, it was completely rebuilt from the original design within the framework of the original walls. The Stations of the Cross are wood carvings from Munich and the high altar is made from Italian marble. The murals are by the Savannah artist, Christopher Murphy (1869-1939), and depict stories from the Old and New Testament.

Twenty of the stained glass windows were designed and executed by glassmakers in Innsbruck, Austria, in the 1880's. Luckily they were not installed until after the fire. The aisle windows represent scenes from the gospels and the lives of the saints. The window of the Blessed Virgin Chapel, is the only window which survived the fire of 1898. The Great Rose Window behind the organ depicts St. Cecilia, patroness of music, with her organ and other instruments.

Colonial Park Cemetery originally lay outside the city wall which stood along what is now Oglethorpe Avenue. Although the "Old Brick Cemetery" had been the vested property of Christ Church since 1758, it functioned as the public burying ground until 1853, except for Jewish citizens, who had their own burial ground on the west side, and the black population. James Habersham, acting governor of the Colony of Georgia; Archibald Bulloch, first governor of the new independent state of Georgia and Button Gwinnett, a signer of the Declaration of Independence (disputed) are buried here.

Oglethorpe Avenue was originally South Broad Street, the southern boundary of the town. The houses on the southern side were built in the early 1820's as the town grew beyond its original confines. "Big Duke" sounded fire alarms from a steel tower that rose high above Colonial Cemetery. Pulitzer Prize-winning author, Conrad Aiken, born in Savannah in 1889, returned to "that most magical of cities" sixty years later to live next door to his childhood home in Nr. 230 Oglethorpe Avenue.

The Owens-Thomas House & Museum, generally considered to be the finest example of Regency architecture in America, was William Jay's first commission in Savannah. Finished in 1819, it was built for Richard Richardson, President of the Savannah Branch of the Bank of the United States. In 1825, the Marquis de Lafayette was housed there. He greeted crowds of Savannahians from the side balcony. Oglethorpe Square (1742) was at first known as Upper New Square.

The Owens-Thomas House & Museum. William Jay was one of the first professional architects in the United States. Before he came from Bath, England, in 1817, houses were built by master builders who were trained as apprentices and worked from books of plans. William Jay, while still in England, designed the house for his cousin by marriage, using Greek architectural details throughout. The young architect's eye for form and proportion is evident in every room.

Reynolds Square, called Lower New Square when it was laid out in 1734, was later named for the first royal governor in Georgia, Captain John Reynolds. Reynolds' first meeting with the assembly of the town was most auspicious, for the Council House on the southeast trust lot collapsed during the meeting. Two years later Reynolds was recalled for mismanaging the affairs of Georgia. The statue of John Wesley is a reminder of another short tenure in the royal colony. The founder of Methodism lived in Savannah from 1736-1738.

The Pink House is one of the few remaining examples of the early wealth of Savannah. This Georgian house was built in 1789 as residence for James Habersham, Jr., a Savannah merchant and political activist. Twenty-two years later it became the Planters Bank; in 1818 the United States Bank; and today it is a restaurant.

The Savannah River. Savannah is the largest foreign commerce port on the South-Atlantic Coast and the farthest inland port on the East Coast. Approximately 1,800 container and break-bulk vessels load and unload their cargo in the Savannah port per year. The upper right picture shows a replica of the *Niña*, one of Columbus' three ships.

The Savannah River seen in early morning haze. The 314-mile river called "the river of the blue waters" by the Indians and "Rio Dulco" by the Spaniards, forms the boundary between Georgia and South Carolina.

The Savannah History Museum, in the Visitor's Center, is located in the old Central of Georgia Railroad terminal (1861). An 1890 4-6-0 steam locomotive sits on the original Central of Georgia tracks in the center of the Savannah History Museum. A film covering Savannah's history from its founding to the present day is shown in the museum's theater.

Central of Georgia Railway Roundhouse & Shops Complex. Built in 1855, it is the oldest and most complete antebellum railroad manufacturing and repair facility still in existence. The exhibits at the Shops include a 27-ton steam locomotive, antique machinery and rolling stock. The photo shows the base of the historic railroad shops' 125-foot-tall smoke stack.

Scarbrough House. William Jay designed this mansion for William Scarbrough, a wealthy English-educated merchant who helped finance the *S.S. Savannah*, the first steamship to cross the Atlantic. Completed in 1819, the mansion became the center of festivities during President Monroe's visit that same year. Unfortunately, three years later the *S.S. Savannah* sank in a gale and William Scarbrough lost his fortune soon after. From 1878-1972, the house operated as a public school for children of African-American descent. The house was restored in 1976 but is not open to the public at present.

First African Baptist Church, traces its roots back to the start of the African-American Baptist Church in Georgia. George Liele, the servant of a British officer, began holding services for a black congregation while the city was occupied during the American Revolution in 1779. In 1782, when American forces retook Savannah, Liele left for Jamaica. His work in Georgia was carried on by his assistant, Andrew Bryan, who preached at a nearby plantation until 1793, when he bought his freedom and a year later erected a house of prayer in Savannah. In 1832, the congregation built this church.

City Market. Four blocks around Ellis Square have been renovated into shops, galleries, restaurants and jazz clubs. Ellis Square was the site of Old City Market which was torn down and replaced by a parking garage in 1954. Ellis Square was laid out in 1733 and named after Henry Ellis who became the second royal governor of Georgia in 1758. Unlike Reynolds, he was tactful and conciliatory and under his capable leadership the colony moved forward, although he stayed for only three years.

Telfair Mansion and Art Museum. Telfair Square (1733), the fourth square laid out by Oglethorpe was the last of the squares to receive its present name. In 1883, St. James Place was renamed for Edward Telfair, a wealthy Scotch merchant and early governor of Georgia. Telfair's son Alexander built the Jay-designed mansion *ca.* 1820. Fifty-five years later his sister Mary bequeathed the home with its furnishings and art collection to the Savannah Historical Society. The Telfair is the oldest public museum in the South. The five Viennese stone statues in front of the portico represent culture.

Isaiah Davenport House Museum was built 1815-1820 by Isaiah Davenport, a Rhode Islander who came to Savannah as a young man. Davenport's skills as a builder, displayed in so-called "Davenport tenements," small, inexpensive clapboard cottages, made him one of Savannah's most sought-after master builders. In his own house Davenport practiced what he had learned as an apprentice in New England and from architectural books. Columbia Square was the eastern city limit when Savannah was a walled city between 1757-90. Bethesda Gate, one of six city gates, was on the square.

There are more houses around the four northeastern squares which date before 1800 than in any other part of Savannah. Immigrants, especially the Irish, and itinerant seamen found inexpensive lodgings in the low-stooped frame houses, duplexes and wooden cottages of this section of the city. This area was considered ill-fated, since many of the epidemics, brought to Savannah by immigrants and sailors, started here.

When the city fathers laid out the four northeastern squares, Warren, Washington (shown here), Columbia, and Greene, between 1791 and 1799, they realized that there was not enough land between the east and west commons (East and West Broad Streets) to allow for six identical wards. Therefore, they decided to place the new, narrower streets closer together and to do away with trust lots, thus creating an atmosphere of a quiet, residential area without high-rising churches or public buildings.

The Pirate's House, dating to 1794, when it was a seafarers' inn, is now a restaurant. A tunnel from the Pirate's House to the river still exists. The Trustees' Garden was located east of Broad Street. Within one month of his arrival, General Oglethorpe established an experimental garden on ten acres on the outskirts of Savannah. Meanwhile the trustees sent botanists to many parts of the world to gather seeds and plants. The first peaches, tender cotton seedlings and medicinal herbs were grown here, as well as some eight thousand mulberry trees for the colony's ill-fated silk production

Emmett Park is named for Irish patriot Robert Emmett. The park contains old harbor lights, a fountain to commemorate three ships named for Savannah and a Vietnam Veterans Memorial. Waving Girl Statue on River Street is a tribute to Florence Martus, the sister of the lighthouse keeper of Elba Island, near Savannah, who for forty-four years waved to passing ships. Sailing ships bound for Savannah for cargo often carried stones as ballast. These stones were used in surfacing the ramps and building walls to contain the sandy slopes.

Ships of the Sea Museum, one of the first waterfront warehouses to be restored, is a maritime museum with a large collection of ship models from the size of a fist to more than eight feet in length. It also contains artifacts, maritime memorabilia and a ship-in-a-bottle collection. Shown on this page is the *S.S. Savannah*, the first steam ship to cross the Atlantic Ocean. It left Savannah on May 22, 1819 for Liverpool, England and arrived there in a record 29 days and 11 hours.

Beach Institute was established in 1865 by the American Missionary Association to educate newly freed slaves. It is now part of the King-Tisdell Cottage Foundation which is dedicated to preserving the African-American history and culture of Savannah. The Beach Institute African-American Cultural Arts Center contains the Ulysses Davis collection of folk art. Shown on this page are two sculptures, "Beast and Beast With Wings," by Ulysses Davis (1913-1990).

King-Tisdell Cottage was built in 1896. Exhibit rooms on the two main floors of the house are used to display art objects and documents relating to African-American history, as well as furniture of the 1890's.

Wormsloe State Historic Site. Noble Jones arrived on the *Anne* with James Edward Oglethorpe. A soldier, constable, member of the royal council and surveyor, Jones built a fortified house in order to guard the seaward approach to Savannah from the South. The tabby ruins (1739), a building material of lime, oyster shells and sand, are the only architectural remnants in Savannah from the first years of the fledgling colony. An alley with over 400 moss-draped oaks leads visitors to a museum, a 3/4 mile-long nature trail, the gravesite of the Jones family and the ruins.

Fort Jackson was built in 1809, on the site of colonial fortifications. Although it saw some action in the War of 1812, the fort was too old and outdated to be of any use in the Civil War. The fort's massive 32-pounder cannon is still being fired on special occasions.

Fort Pulaski, was built between 1829 and 1847, to protect the coastline from invasion. Its 7-foot-thick brick walls and 48-foot moat were regarded impregnable. However, in April 1862, during the first and last battle the fort ever saw, the U.S. Army's new rifled guns blasted holes two feet deep into the masonry and exposed the fort's magazine within a day, forcing the 385-man garrison to surrender. Fort Pulaski is a National Monument and is operated by the National Park Service.

Tybee Lighthouse is the oldest and tallest in Georgia. The bottom sixty feet date from 1773, the upper ninety-four feet from 1867. The walls are twelve feet thick at the bottom and taper to 18 inches at the top. The room at the base of the lighthouse was used for storage. The lens at the top magnifies a 1000 watt bulb, so that it can be seen 18 miles away. The buildings around the lighthouse date from between ca 1800 to 1885, they were used to house the keepers and as storage rooms.

Thunderbolt Harbor on the Wilmington River (Intracoastal Waterway), originally an Indian village, was started by the early settlers as a fort with earthen breastworks and a battery of four cannons to protect Savannah from the east. Thunderbolt derives its name from a bolt of lightening which hit the ground and caused a spring of clear water to gush forth. The harbor is the center of Savannah's shrimping industry and the site of the annual Blessing of the Fleet in June.

Hofwyl-Broadfield Plantation. Around 1807, William Brailsford of Charleston used slave labor to clear cypress swamps on the Altamaha River, built earthen dikes and irrigation ditches, and began the cultivation of rice. His plantation, Broadfield, comprised of 7,300 acres, several homes and 357 slaves. His granddaughter Ophelia Dent moved to an adjacent plantation, Hofwyl, named after a Suisse school her husband attended. The present Hofwyl house was built in the late 1850's. The plantation's fortune declined after the Civil War, but the Dent family continued to produce rice until 1915.

Fort Frederica, was built by General Oglethorpe in 1736 to protect the colony from a Spanish invasion. The military town, named for the king's only son Frederick, consisted of a tabby fort, 84 lots for settlers and barracks for the soldiers. It was surrounded by a wall and a moat. At the time of the Battle of Bloody Marsh, when Oglethorpe and his 650 men defeated a Spanish column of over 3000 men, the civilian population of Frederica reached about 500. The regiment was disbanded in 1749. The townspeople, unable to survive without the soldiers, moved away, and Frederica fell to ruin.

Lighthouse Museum, St. Simons Island. The Museum of Coastal History is housed in the former lighthouse keeper's cottage (1872).

Jekyll Island was named by Oglethorpe for Sir Joseph Jekyll who had contributed generously to the Georgia venture. An outpost of Fort Frederica in colonial days, Jekyll Island was originally owned by a Brunswick merchant, du Bignon, who sold it in 1886 to the newly-formed Jekyll Island Club as a retreat for wealthy Northerners. Millionaires such as Rockefeller and Morgan built their mansion-sized homes, called "cottages," on the west side of the island. Since buying the island in 1947, the State of Georgia has renovated some of the cottages and opened them as house-museums.

SAVANNAH - EL PASADO Y EL PRESENTE

El 12 de febrero de 1733 una pequeña galera británica, llevando a su bordo 114 colonos, echaba el ancla al pie de un alto farallón en el río Savannah. James Edward Oglethorpe, uno de los fideicomisarios de la colonia que había asumido el liderazgo de los mismos, había elegido la meseta de 13 metros de altura para establecer allí la capital de la 13ª colonia de Inglaterra. Oglethorpe era miembro del Parlamento y había concebido la idea de una nueva colonia en que los colonos fueran gente pobre, soldados y protestantes extranjeros.

Además de ser un refugio para los pobres el nuevo asentamiento serviría de defensa entre los prósperos territorios de la Carolina y las posesiones españolas en Florida, y abastecería a Inglaterra en seda, lino, potasa y vino. A cambio de su transporte gratuito a la colonia, de unas 20 hectáreas de tierra (incluyendo una pequeña parcela en la ciudad para construcción de una casa), de ganado y de pertrechos, los colonos tenían que comprometerse a permanecer en Georgia durante un mínimo de tres años, y contribuir a la defensa de la colonia.

En vista de los problemas que se les presentaban por estar mal equipados para hacer frente a unas tierras salvajes, y no a la tierra prometida, hubo colonos desilusionados que comenzaron a abandonar Georgia para acudir a las Carolinas, en donde no se les prohibía ser propietarios de esclavos o tierras, ni tampoco el beber y vender ron. En 1743 Oglethorpe regresó a Inglaterra para no volver, dejando tras de sí una colonia desanimada y muy reducida. El golpe final se produjo cuando, en 1751, el Parlamento cortó todos los fondos para la 13ª colonia. Un año después los Fideicomisarios devolvieron su Carta a la Corona.

La primera bonanza de Savannah se basó en el cultivo del arroz, un trabajo de mano de obra intensiva que requería el uso de esclavos ya que los pantanos eran considerados „como tierra no apta para que el hombre blanco trabajara en ellos."

En 1750, en los 15 años despues de haberse abolido la ley anti-esclavista de los fideicomisarios, el número total de esclavos en la colonia ascendía a unos 15.000. Surgió una nueva clase de ricos plantadores y armadores que construyeron grandes propiedades y elegantes casas urbanas. Los almacenes a lo largo de la Bahía estaban repletos de arroz, añil, madera, pieles y los primeros fardos de un nuevo cultivo, el algodón, para ser expedidos a Bristol o Liverpool.

Durante los últimos años de la aventura británica en el Nuevo Mundo, Savannah se convirtió en una ciudad dividida. Mientras los viejos colonos defendían firmemente al gobernador real y las leyes británicas, sus hijos se reunían en la Taberna de Tondee para hablar de insurrección, auto determinación, boicot y libertad. El 10 de agosto de 1776, los „Liberty Boys" y los ciudadanos exaltados de Savannah celebraron la Declaración de Independencia con un cortejo funerario en burla del Rey Jorge.

Dos años despues, los británicos reconquistaron Savannah en un solo día y Georgia se convirtió de nuevo en una provincia real británica, aunque ciertas partes del interior y de la costa meridional siguieron en manos de los insurrectos. En Octubre de 1779, una flota francesa bajo el mando de Charles, Conde d'Estaing, desembarcó más de 4.000 soldados a los que pronto se unieron fuerzas norteamericanas desde Augusta. En su tentativa, fallida, de reconquistar Savannah, se libró una de las batallas más sangrientas de la Revolución. La liberación de Savannah se produjo finalmente en 1782.

El invento de la desmotadora de algodón por un joven maestro de escuela de New Haven, Eli Whitney, transformó a Savannah convirtiéndola en puerto mundial. En 1790 las exportaciones de algodón sumaron 1.000 balas.

Treinta años despues eran de 90.000 balas y en 1840 habían ascendido a 408.000 balas por año.

En vísperas de la Guerra Civil la ciudad tenía una población de 14.000 habitantes. Una serie de mansiones majestuosas y de casas unidas elegantes daban a las nuevas calles cerca del Parque Forsyth un aire de prosperidad y de elegancia. Tres línas de ferrocarril transportaban el algodón y la madera de las tierras de Georgia a los almacenes sitos sobre el río Savannah.

El 19 de enero de 1861 Georgia se convirtió en el quinto Estado en separarse de los Estados Unidos. Savannah se sentía invencible ya que dos semanas antes una pequeña banda de voluntarios había capturado el Fuerte Pulaski, en la desembocadura del río Savannah. Un año despues, cuando la Unión reconquistó el Fuerte, los savannahianos comenzaron a darse cuenta de que el bloqueo de su puerto por la Unión representaba el fin del comercio y de los negocios, y de que los ingleses y franceses no echarían tanto de menos el algodón como para venir en su ayuda. Los almacenes se cerraron, los galpones del puerto permanecieron vacíos y solamente alguno que otro desafiante del bloqueo echaba el ancla en River Street. De no ser por las tropas de guarnición en Savannah la ciudad se hubiera convertido en una ciudad fantasma. Despues de la Batalla de Atlanta unos 9.000 grises estaban a la espera del ejército de la Unión de 70.000 hombres. Cuando se vió claro que todas las rutas de abastecimiento de Savannah estaban en manos del enemigo, abandonaron las defensas de la ciudad y Savannah se rindió.

La Guerra Civil dejó a Savannah convertida en una ciudad derrotada, con sus bellas plazas y mansiones estropeadas y envejecidas, con el puerto bloqueado por buques de la Confederación hundidos, con el ferrocarril destruído y sin empleos: no había comida, no había dinero.

Ya para 1883 Savannah se había recuperado lo suficiente como para celebrar su sesquicentenario con luces eléctricas, tranvías, algunas casas con instalaciones sanitarias, y por encima de todo, con una Bolsa del Algodón, recientemente inaugurada, que pronto pasó a ser denominada la „Wall Street del Sur". La ciudad se extendió al sur de la Calle Gaston, añadiendo el Distrito Victoriano con su arquitectura rebuscada a los muchos estilos de Savannah. Los fines de semana los habitantes tomaban el nuevo ferrocarril hasta la Playa de Tybas, o acudían a los conciertos en el Parque Forsyth, o iban a las regatas o carreras de caballos. El nuevo canal dragado en el río hizo de Savannah un puerto de importancia en la costa atlántica.

La Primera Guerra Mundial cambió en forma espectacular la tranquilidad de la ciudad al convertirse el puerto de Savannah en uno de los principales puertos de embarque. Esta situación se prolongó durante la Segunda Guerra Mundial, cuando los gigantescos bombarderos de la Octava Fuerza Aérea despegaban del Aeródromo Hunter, del Ejército, para destruir a las fuerzas de Hitler.

Despues de la guerra Savannah cayó de nuevo en la decadencia y muchas de sus hermosas casas se transformaron en casas de vecindad de barrios bajos. Sin embargo, en la década de 1950 ocurrió algo que conmovió a Savannah. Se demolió el antiguo Mercado Municipal para dar lugar a un garage de estacionamiento: los ciudadanos, sintiendose ofendidos, se movilizaron para salvar el distrito histórico antes de perderlo a manos de los demoledores. En 1966 el Servicio Nacional de Parques designó una zona de dos millas y media como Patrimonio Nacional.

Durante los Juegos Olímpicos del Centenario, en 1996, Savannah una vez más será objeto de la atención mundial. Los concursos olímpicos de yates se llevarán a cabo en el Océano Atlántico, y el „volley-ball" de playa, deporte olímpico por primera vez, atraerá a unos 8.000 espectadores a la cercana Isla Tybee.

Index — Savannah

LEGEND: Interesting and fun for children of all ages

 Access for handicapped people

 Partial access and/or with assistance

For sites on walking tours, follow pictures and captions in book and page numbers and colored tours on map.
The distances and directions for driving tours are from the corner of Bay and Bull Streets.

Tour #1 (Red): HISTORIC SAVANNAH
A walking tour from the northern (Savannah River) to the
southern boundary (Forsyth Park) of Historic Savannah.

Page

9 Christ Episcopal Church
28 Bull Street at Johnson Square
Tel.: (912) 232-4131
Hours: Tues. and Fri. 10:30-3:30
Admission: No

12, 13 Juliette Gordon Low Birthplace
142 Bull Street
Tel.: (912) 233-4501
Hours: Mon. - Sat. 10-4, Sun. 12:30-4:30
(closed Wednesdays)
Admission: Yes

18, 19 Green-Meldrim House
Madison Square
Tel.: (912) 233-3845
Hours: Tues., Thurs., Fri. 10-4 (closed Dec. 15 - Jan. 15
and 2 weeks before Easter)
Admission: Donation

21 Temple Mickve Israel Museum
20 East Gordon Street (entrance E. Wayne St.)
Tel.: (912) 233-1547
Hours: Mon. - Fri. 10-12, 2-4
Admission: Donation

Page

26 Massie Heritage Interpretation Center
207 East Gordon Street on Calhoun Square
Tel.: (912) 651-7380
Hours: Mon. - Fri. 9-4:40
Admission: Donation

28, 29 Andrew Low House
329 Abercorn Street on Lafayette Square
Tel.: (912) 233-6854
Hours: Mon. - Sat. 10:30-4, Sun. 12-4
(closed Thursdays)
Admission: Yes

30 Hamilton-Turner House
330 Abercorn on Lafayette Square
Tel.: (912) 233-4800
Hours: Daily 10-6
Admission: Yes

Flannery O'Connor
Childhood Home (not shown)
207 E. Charlton Street on Lafayette Square
Hours: Friday, Saturday and Sunday, 1-4 p.m.
Admission: No

31-33   Cathedral of St. John the Baptist   ♿
Abercorn at Harris Street
Tel.: (912) 233-4709
Hours: Daily
Admission: No

Page
36, 37   The Owens-Thomas House & Museum
124 Abercorn Street on Oglethorpe Square
Tel.: (912) 233-9743
Hours: Tues. - Sat. 10-4:30,
Sun. & Mon. 2-4:30 (closed January)
Admission: Yes

TOUR #2 (Green): HISTORIC SAVANNAH

A walking tour from the western to the eastern boundary of Historic Savannah.
(M.L. King, Jr., Blvd., originally West Broad Street to East Broad Street)

Page
42   The Savannah History Museum   ♿ 🧒
and Savannah Visitors Center
303 Martin Luther King, Jr., Blvd.
Tel.: (912) 238-1779
Hours: Daily 9-5
Admission: Yes

43   Roundhouse Complex   ♿ 🧒
601 West Harris Street (one block south
of Visitors Center)
Tel.: (912) 238-1779
Hours: Fri. - Tues. 11-4:30
Admission: Yes

45   First African Baptist Church
23 Montgomery Street on Franklin Square
Tel.: (912) 233-6597
Hours: Mon. - Thurs. by appointment, Fri. 10-2
Admission: No

Page
47   Telfair Mansion and Art Museum   ♿
121 Barnard Street on Telfair Square
Tel.: (912) 232-1177
Hours: Tues. - Sat. 10-5, Sun. 2-5
(closed Mondays)
Admission: Yes

48   Isaiah Davenport House   ♿
324 East State Street on Columbia Square
Tel.: (912) 236-8097
Hours: Mon. - Sat. 10-4:30, Sun. 1:30-4:30
(closed Thursdays)
Admission: Yes

53   Ships of the Sea Museum   ♿ 🧒
503 East River Street & 504 East Bay Street
Tel.: (912) 232-1511
Hours: Daily 10-5
Admission: Yes

TOUR #3 (Blue): AFRICAN-AMERICAN HERITAGE TOUR

A walking tour.

Page
42   The Savannah History Museum   ♿ 🧒
303 Martin Luther King, Jr., Blvd.
Tel.: (912) 238-1779
Hours: Daily 9-5
Admission: Yes

Page
45   First African Baptist Church
23 Montgomery Street on Franklin Square
Tel.: (912) 233-6597
Hours: Mon. - Thurs. by appointment, Fri. 10-2
Admission: No

Page

18, 19 Green-Meldrim House
Madison Square
Tel.: (912) 233-3845
Hours: Tues., Thurs., Fri. 10-4
(closed Dec. 15 - Jan. 15 and
2 weeks before Easter)
Admission: Donation

54 Beach Institute African-American
Cultural Arts Center
502 East Harris Street
Tel.: (912) 234-8000
Hours: Tues. - Sun. 12-5
Admission: Donation

Page

55 King-Tisdell Cottage
514 East Huntington Street
Tel.: (912) 234-8000
Hours: Mon. - Fri. 10:30-4:30,
Sat. & Sun. 1-4
Admission: Yes

TOUR #4: WORMSLOE HISTORIC SITE, AQUARIUM AND SCIENCE MUSEUM
A driving tour.

Go south on Abercorn (4.7 miles), turn left on DeRenne Ave. (2.1 miles, right on Skidaway Road (3 miles) to

Page

56 Wormsloe State Historic Site
7601 Skidaway Road, Isle of Hope
Tel.: (912) 352-2548
Hours: Tues. - Sat. 9-5, Sun. 2-5:30
Admission: Yes

Return on Skidaway Road (0.5 miles), turn left on Ferguson Ave. (2.3 miles). You will pass Bethesda Home for Boys built in 1740 by Reverend Whitefield, left on Diamond Causeway (3.6 miles), then left on McWhorter Dr. (4.2 miles) to

Aquarium (not shown)
The University of Georgia Marine
Extension Service
McWhorter Drive, Skidaway Island
Tel.: (912) 598-3474   598-3974
Hours: Mon. - Fri. 9-4, Sat. & Sun 12-5
Admission: Donation

Return to Diamond Causeway which becomes Water Street (8.7 miles), turn left on 63rd Street, right on Paulson Street to

Savannah Science Museum (not shown)
4405 Paulsen Street near 63rd Street
Tel.: (912) 355-6705
Hours: Tues. - Sat. 10-5, Sun. 2-5
Planetarium: Sun. at 3 p.m.
Admission: Yes

To return to Historic District continue on Paulson, turn left on Victory Drive (0.7 miles), right on Abercorn Street.

TOUR #5: FORTS, TYBEE ISLAND
A driving tour.

Go east on Bay Street, left on President Street Extension (2.7 miles), turn left on Fort Jackson Road (1.3 miles) bear right to

Page

57   Old Fort Jackson
     1 Fort Jackson Road
     Tel.: (912) 232-3945
     Hours: Mon. - Sat. 9-5
     Admission: Yes

Continue on President Street Extension (3 miles) Turn right at sign of the environmental education center to

     Oatland Island Education Center (not shown)
     711 Sandtown Road
     Tel.: (912) 897-3773
     Hours: Mon.-Fri. 8:30-5
     Admission: 1 can of dog food per person or cash donation

Return to President Street Extension, continue east (0.5 miles), turn left on US 80 east (7.5 miles) to

58   Fort Pulaski
     Cockspur Island
     Tel.: (912) 786-5787
     Hours: Daily 8:30-5:30
     Admission: Yes

Continue on US 80 east (1.8 miles), turn left on Bryan Avenue (blinking light), left on Van Horne Ave., right on Meddin Drive to

59   Tybee Lighthouse   Fort Screven and Tybee Museum
     Meddin Drive   (not shown)
     Tel.: (912) 786-5801   Meddin Drive
     Hours: Mon. - Fri. 10-6, (winter weekdays 12-4)   Tel.: (912) 786-4077
     Sat. & Sun. 10-4 (closed Tuesdays)   Hours: Daily 10-6 (winter 1-5)
     Admission: Yes   Admission: Yes

To return to the Historic District take US 80 west (15 miles) to Thunderbolt (page 60), continue on US 80 which becomes Victory Drive (2.8 miles), turn right on Abercorn Street. Don't miss beautiful Victory Drive, especially when azaleas are in bloom.

TOUR #6: COAST AND GOLDEN ISLES
A driving tour.

Go I-16 W (12 miles), then I-95 S (56.5 miles), exit #9, turn left on GA 99 (1.4 miles), turn right on US 17, entrance on the left to

Page

61   Hofwyl-Broadfield Plantation
State Historic Site
US 17
Tel.: (912) 264-9263
Hours: Tues. - Sat. 9-5, Sun. 2-5:30
Admission: Yes

Go south on US 17 (11 miles), turn left onto Brunswick-St. Simons Causeway (4.6 miles), left on Sea Island Road (2.5 miles), left on Frederica Road (3 miles) to

62   Fort Frederica National Monument
Frederica Road, St. Simons Island
Tel.: (912) 638-3639
Hours: Daily 8-6 (winter 8-5), Visitor Center daily 9-6 (winter 9-5)
Admission: Yes (per vehicle)

Return on Frederica Road (5.4 miles), left on Demere Road - you will pass Bloody Marsh Battle Site (National Park Service) to

63   Lighthouse and Museum of Coastal History
101 12th Street, St. Simons Island
Tel.: (912) 638-4666
Hours: Tues. - Fri. 9:30-5, Sat. 10-5, Sun. 1:30-5
Admission: Yes

Return to US 17, continue south, turn left on Jekyll Island Causeway. Pay toll at entrance ($2.00), left U-turn after 0.3 miles, turn right on N. Riverview Road, bear right at fork onto Stable Road to

64   Jekyll Island National Historic Landmark District, Orientation Center
Stable Road
Tel.: (912) 635-2762 or 635-2119
Hours: Daily 9:30-4, Tram tours daily 10-3 on the hour (includes
tour of historic "cottages.") Length of tour: 1½ hours
Admission: Yes

BOOKS BY CITIES IN COLOR, INC.

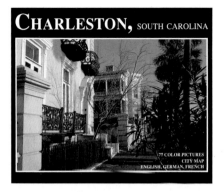

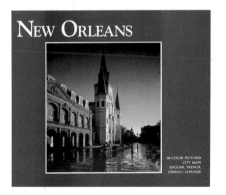

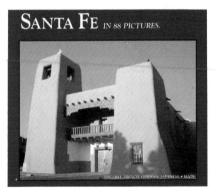

A GUIDE TO ANTEBELLUM GEORGIA
(To be published 1995)

Also Available:
Vienna, Austria,
Rio de Janeiro, Brazil

Cities in Color, Inc.
Lisa D. Hoff
12 Braemore Drive, N.W.
Atlanta, GA 30328-4844
Tel.: 404 255-1185 • Fax: 404 252 7218